TURBO-CHARGE & TRANSFORM!

Turbo-charge & Transform!

Leadership team brainstorming blasts for awesome innovation

Ellen M. Huxtable

With greatest appreciation to Bob and Nathan
for their support
and to
Lynn Zuk-Lloyd, Paul Lloyd,
William and Susan Price
for their encouragement and ideas

TABLE OF CONTENTS

INTRODUCTION

CONCLUSION

INTRODUCTION

What if you had a structured format to generate innovative ideas and quickly translate these ideas into action? What if you could hold a corporate retreat, with real progress, during a one-hour management meeting? What if the systems to accomplish this were available on simple worksheets you could use whenever you wanted?

Welcome to Turbo-charge & Transform! a process to help your team strategize, plan and implement effective change. Turbo-charge and Transform! adapts to your needs and your agenda. Each unit consists of an overview, a guide to the unit and a worksheet. The exercises can be used individually or as a sequenced program, and can be integrated into your regularly scheduled meetings or form the basis for a separate event.

Choose the units that fit your needs, when you need them. Boost the impact of your management meetings. Spark quick brainstorming sessions or engage in serious strategic planning. Explore the possibilities and get set to Turbo-charge and Transform! your business today!

UNIT 1: A FOCUS ON MISSION, VISION AND VALUES

Innovation is a two-edged sword. It can be the lifeblood and salvation of your business, or it can lead to irreparable disaster. Innovation can move you toward your goals or it can lead to unproductive and costly dead ends. No one has resources to waste. So how do you focus your team efforts toward achieving productive innovation?

Establishing a common vision can be a critical first step. Leadership must share a common vision in order to focus on a common goal. What is your company all about? What are your goals? What are your values? What are you trying to achieve? A discussion on these concepts may reveal a surprising divergence of opinions. All ideas may be valid, but they might point the company in contradictory directions for the future. Taking the time upfront to reach consensus on these key issues can save hours of frustration and rework as you plan and implement programs for the future. .

Reaching consensus can take time and effort. Input from a variety of team members can enrich the discussion and elicit new, dynamic ideas. Open discussions can also create a sense of ownership and promote participation. Consensus may be achieved through discussion and negotiation, or top management may dictate the direction. Whichever course is taken, all players must have a clear understanding of the basic company values and goals, and must be committed to wholeheartedly supporting these.

Compounding the challenge of reaching consensus is the reality that we exist in a dynamically changing world. A successful organization must have the flexibility to adapt and change course smoothly and quickly, with all components transitioning as one. Tomorrow's targets may be very different from the ones we establish today. However, at any one time, leadership team members must have a common concept and be working toward common goals.

GUIDE TO UNIT 1

Purpose:

This unit encourages the team to focus on the mission, vision and values of the organization, promotes reflection on these issues and helps assess the need for revision, reminders or explanations.

Objectives:

- Promote discussion
- Evaluate statements for relevance
- Identify and help address conflicting perceptions
- Promote understanding
- Suggest additions, changes and modifications
- Identify needs for communication

Process:

1. Select and assign the exercise. This may be done in advance or during the team meeting.
2. Ask team members to complete the form to the best of their knowledge and experience. Not all items have to be answered.
3. Discuss the answers to the individual items.
    Do you have an official statement of mission, vision and values?
    If so, how closely does reality match the official statement?
    What are the variances between responses and the official statement? Are these material?
    Is your statement relevant to current conditions?
    Do you need to develop or refine your statements?
4. This exercise can be done in one session or extended over as many sessions as needed.

Follow-up:

- Reflect on the discussion and bring additional ideas or thoughts to the next meeting, for further discussion and exploration.
- Review and consider revisions to your focus and statement.

WORKSHEET 1
A FOCUS ON MISSION, VISION AND VALUES

Company Name: _____ Today's Date: _____

Participant's Name: _____

Our Industry: _____

Our Corporate Mission:

Our Corporate Vision:

Our Corporate Values:

WORKSHEET 1
A FOCUS ON MISSION, VISION AND VALUES

My thoughts and ideas on our mission:

My thoughts and ideas on our vision:

My thoughts and ideas on our values:

Areas for future consideration:

UNIT 2: MISSION, VISION AND VALUES STATEMENT

What are your mission, vision and values? Do you have a formal statement? If so, is it current? Does it meet your needs now and into the future, or does it reflect an outdated reality?

A current, carefully structured mission, vision and values statement is the touchstone for management decisions in every area. It is especially critical during times of transition, change and innovation. It helps guide resources toward promoting the goals of your organization. Every leadership team member as well as every employee should know, understand and support your mission, vision and values.

Where do you begin? If you have a current statement, review it. Does it accurately and fully express your position and beliefs? Consider its applicability in your present context. Will this statement support and inspire your team now and into the future?

If you do not have a statement, begin by discussing your values and goals. What is important to you? How do you want to conduct business? What do you hope to achieve for the organization and for society at large? What is your really big vision for the future?

Invite input from a range of individuals. Sometimes the clearest vision comes from unexpected sources. New and long-term employees, vendors and customers may provide perspectives and ideas that capture the essence of your organization.

Take time to let ideas develop. Carefully select the words you use. Strive to capture both the power and nuances of your organization. Look to the future. Does your statement inspire? Is it memorable? Does it capture the essence of your organization or does it sound like a generic platitude?

Finalize your statement and disseminate it. Do the best you can, but do not hold out for perfection, because perfection is perpetually elusive. Let everyone in your organization know your mission, vision and values statement, and discuss its applicability to every aspect of your business. Let the statement become a living, dynamic part of everyday business.

Finally, revisit your statement regularly. Update and tweak it as necessary, but strive to maintain the core concepts and values as constants. Strive to become an organization that is centered, focused and inspired by its mission, vision and values.

GUIDE TO UNIT 2

Purpose:

> Distill and express your mission, vision and values. Your mission, vision and values will set the direction and tone of all aspect of your business.

Objectives:

- Promote discussion and exploration of the statements.
- Revise statements as indicated.
- Clarify the intent and meaning of the statements.
- Capture the statements so they may serve as guides for future innovative activity.

Process:

1. Select and assign the exercise. This may be done in advance or during the team meeting.
2. Discuss the company's mission, vision and values, both as expressed in any current statements, and as perceived by team members. What possible changes come to mind?
3. Depending on specific circumstances, you may want to set parameters for the range or types of change that will be considered.
4. Through discussion, gain consensus on recommended modifications.
5. Work as a group to refine the language and tone.
6. This exercise can be done in one session or extended over as many sessions as needed.

Follow-up:

- Share the final statement throughout the organization.
- Discuss the process followed and the rationale for decisions made.
- Revisit the statement periodically and revise it as needed.
- Use the statement to help make decisions and choices as you take innovative action.

WORKSHEET 2
MISSION, VISION AND VALUES STATEMENT

Company Name: _____   Today's Date: _____

Our current mission, vision and values statement and/or core ideals:

Strong points in our statement:

Things to change or add to our statement:

Our new mission statement:

UNIT 3: SETTING A BASELINE FOR INNOVATION

Business today is dramatically different from yesterday. How does your organization fit into the current reality? Realistically, given your past and present, what does the future look like? Are you changing as rapidly as your environment? Are you comfortably ahead of the curve, competing in the middle of the curve, or lagging behind? What are your prospects? What opportunities do you see emerging? What threats are on the horizon? What are you doing about them?

Ask as many questions as you can. You should have many more questions than answers. Without getting bogged down by details or agonizing over answers, brainstorm on a broad picture of the future, and the position and role of your organization within that new reality. Don't be afraid to raise issues. It is far better to raise hypothetical challenges than to deal with unexpected crises.

Once you have completed your vision of the future with all the detail you can muster, discuss the implications, the challenges and the opportunities. Identify key areas for action and begin to proactively address these. Do not be dismayed if you lack the time and resources to address every issue; the number of issues is always far greater than the available resources. However, by identifying the issues critical to your organization and acting on even a select few of these, you are strategically improving your competitive position.

GUIDE TO UNIT 3

Purpose:

- Explore team members' perceptions of key components of the business, including its mission, status, goals and future.
- Highlight areas which might benefit from in-depth exploration.
- Suggest which Turbo-charge & Transform! units might be most applicable for future meetings.

Objectives:

- Promote discussion
- Identify and help address conflicting perceptions
- Solicit input
- Identify opportunities
- Build camaraderie

Process:

1. Select and assign the exercise. This may be done in advance or during the team meeting.
2. Ask team members to complete the form to the best of their knowledge and experience. Not all items have to be answered.
3. Discuss the answers to the individual items.
   a. Where is there a consensus of opinion?
   b. Where are there discrepancies?
   c. What suggestions are made?
   d. What ideas are generated by the group?
   e. What next steps should the group take?
4. Option: The group can focus only on selected questions; not all questions need to be addressed concurrently.
5. This exercise can be done in one session or extended over as many sessions as needed.

Follow-up:

- Reflect on the discussion and bring additional ideas or thoughts to the next meeting, for further discussion and exploration.
- Explore selected ideas from the session for immediate action.
- Select specific units in the Turbo-charge & Transform! series to address identified issues and opportunities.

WORKSHEET 3
SETTING A BASELINE FOR INNOVATION

Company Name: _____   Today's Date: _____

Participant's Name: _____

Our Industry: _____

Our Mission, Vision and Values:

Our Status:

Our Future Prospects:

Our Goals:

What challenges do we face?

What new challenges do we expect?

What opportunities do we have?

What are we doing about these?

UNIT 4: SWOT
STRENGTHS, WEAKNESSES, OPPORTUNITIES, THREATS

SWOT is a classic strategic exercise, focusing on the potentially positive and negative factors an organization faces, both internally and externally.

- Strengths are the internal positive attributes. These can include a strong financial position, top notch staff, desirable patents, etc.

- Weaknesses are the internal negative factors. Examples of these might be the lack of a succession plan, outdated machinery or a non-competitive wage structure.

- Opportunities are positive situations in the external environment. An expected huge increase in the demand for your products and the opening of new market channels are examples of opportunities.

- Threats are external negative situations which jeopardize your position. A strong new competitor entering your area, new legislation which is detrimental to you and shrinking demand for your products are all potential threats.

Brainstorm on the strengths, weaknesses, opportunities and threats envisioned by team members. This can be done by either concentrating on one area at a time, or working in all four areas concurrently. All ideas should be captured; do not limit input by criticizing, critiquing or arguing over the validity of observations.

Once all ideas are captured, evaluate your position. Discuss options for your organization to capitalize on strengths and opportunities and minimize or neutralize weaknesses and threats. You may also be able to identify strategies for converting a weakness into a strength or a threat into an opportunity.

A SWOT analysis can serve as a quick and effective snapshot of your competitive position. It can help identify changes you can make to improve your edge in the marketplace, and generate dialogue on taking proactive action.

GUIDE TO UNIT 4

Purpose:

SWOT assesses the internal and external environments for strengths, weaknesses, opportunities and threats.

Objectives:

- Identify areas of SWOT for the company.
- Prioritize them and identify critical areas.
- Develop strategies to turn these into opportunities.
- Take action to address these issues.

Process:

1. Select and assign the exercise.
2. Review definitions of SWOT, as described on the worksheet.
3. Have team members list items in each area of SWOT. Keep the discussion open-ended and non-judgmental. The objective at this time is to capture all ideas and opinions.
4. Review the areas of SWOT and identify critical or key items to address.
5. Ask team members to suggest items for the right hand column, that is, how can the areas of SWOT be effectively handled.
6. Prioritize areas for action.
7. Note that some areas that are not high priority may have simple solutions which can be easily implemented. You may choose to address these areas immediately and get them resolved. This can also build momentum to tackle some of the more complex issues.
8. Assign tasks for follow-up.

Follow-up:

1. Have progress reports at the next meeting.
2. Assess progress and make new assignments as needed.
3. Tackle additional projects once the first items have been resolved.

WORKSHEET 4
SWOT

Strengths: Internal factors in our favor.	How can we maximize their impact?

Weaknesses: Internal factors which put us at a disadvantage	How can we minimize their impact?

Notes:

Opportunities: External options for gain	How can we take advantage of these?

Threats: External challenges	How can we neutralize these?

Notes:

UNIT 5: ENVISIONING THE CHANGING UNIVERSE

What does the future hold? One thing is for certain; like it or not, there will be change. Change can be a challenge, it can spell disaster, or it can be the catalyst for awesome opportunities. Change can take us by surprise. We can pretend it doesn't exist and try to ignore it, or we can expect, anticipate and welcome it. Change may cut off some markets, but for every lost opportunity other options are created, for those creative enough to see them. These new opportunities not only can replace lost markets, but indeed some opportunities can position a business to succeed and grow rapidly into the future.

Change is occurring at all levels of our experience. Global trends in the economy, natural resources and international politics have far-reaching repercussions. National and local dynamics likewise influence our markets. Customers, competitors and participants in the supply chain are adapting and responding to a roller coaster of change. Ground rules are constantly shifting, as competitors jockey for an advantage and customers react to new realities. In the midst of this, organizations are called upon to envision the future marketplace and take steps to secure a strong competitive position.

Consider change at the global level. What trends do you see? What is the probability of them continuing into the future? Some things such as an aging population can reasonably expected to continue, while other trends such as those in fashion are likely to be short lived. Consider change in various sectors - financial, social, economic, political, ecologic and more. How will the various trends compliment or compete with each other? What do you predict as the net result?

Next, consider national, regional and local trends. Are these consistent or inconsistent with the global patterns? Again, consider trends across multiple sectors. What inferences can you draw? How do you predict the dynamics will resolve? What impact will the various identified trends have on your organization? What is the probability?

What actions can you take now to respond to your vision of the future? Given other considerations such as cost and risk, what options do you want to implement? Identify key activities and structure and implement appropriate actions. Change is occurring with unprecedented rapidity. Strategize, plan and begin implementing your responses now to meet future opportunities and address future challenges.

GUIDE TO UNIT 5

Purpose:

Observe changes in the global and local environments, project trends and create strategic, innovative responses to these for the organization.

Objectives:

- Share observations and projections regarding future trends.
- Identify critical trends.
- Project their impact on the immediate business environment.
- Project their impact on the company.
- Identify and implement key strategic solutions.

Process:

1. Select and assign the exercise.
2. Set the ground rule that all opinions are valid and will be respected.
3. Record observations in appropriate cells.
4. Not all cells need to be filled and there can be multiple points in each cell.
5. Expand the chart as needed.
6. Discuss responses and identify key elements.
7. Project their impact on the business.
8. Discuss strategies to address these issues.
9. Take strategic action as indicated.

Follow-up:

1. Have progress reports at the next meeting.
2. Assess progress and make new assignments as needed.
3. You may want to tackle additional projects once the first items have been resolved.
4. Repeat the exercise periodically to assess changes in the environment and expected future scenarios.

WORKSHEET 5
ENVISIONING THE CHANGING UNIVERSE

	International / National	Local	Our Company
Environment			
Economy			
Technology			
Demographics			
Political			
Cultural			
Our Industry			
Our Customers			
Our Competitors			
Other:			

	New Opportunities	New Projects	Next Steps
Environment			
Economy			
Technology			
Demographics			
Political			
Cultural			
Our Industry			
Our Customers			
Our Competitors			
Other:			

UNIT 6: RESPONDING TO THE CHANGING UNIVERSE

Organizations today are facing overwhelming change. The scope of challenges and opportunities can be immobilizing. "Too much information" is the watchword for a whole generation. Yet in the midst of this, leaders are called upon to make decisions and implement programs that will not just respond to change, but anticipate and meet change head on.

The dynamics of the process are complex. While executive leadership demands a visionary, "big picture" perspective, this alone is inadequate for success. Transformation requires action and action requires focus. Productive activity demands a shift from a global perspective to the analytic, and from the analytic to the pragmatic. From the universe of possibilities, leaders must have the capacity to select a critical issue, assess the associated opportunity or threat, develop options and select and implement a reasonable course of action.

As a project moves from concept to implementation, the input of different stakeholders can be the key to success or failure. The front line employee may raise issues totally unforeseen by management. The staff accountant may point out unexpected costs or savings. A few words with potential customers or suppliers may upend basic assumptions. A summary of the proposed project can be a valuable tool as the project is defined and ultimately implemented.

In a large organization, the process is further complicated by the relationships between departments, divisions and units. A change or innovation in one area can have unexpected repercussions which must be addressed elsewhere in the organization. A seemingly simple project can take on a life of its own, as other areas scramble to adapt. Document changes and discuss them in advance to minimize surprises and keep projects on track.

Implementing change requires vision, focus and attention to detail. Consider all stakeholders and solicit their input to develop your program for change.

GUIDE TO UNIT 6

Purpose:

Focus on a critical change element, review options and plan actions.

Objectives:

- Promote discussion regarding perceived trends and their impact on the company.
- Explore opportunities, challenges and options.
- Examine the impact on stakeholders and within the organization.
- Identify actions to be taken.

Process:

1. Select and assign the exercise.
2. Set the ground rule that all opinions are valid and will be respected.
3. Provide time for participants to record their opinions.
4. Discuss responses and identify key elements.
5. Decide on a preferred option.
6. Discuss the impact on stakeholders and the organization.
7. Do additional research as necessary.
8. Identify actions to be taken and assign deadlines and accountabilities.

Follow-up:

1. Have progress reports at the next meeting.
2. Assess progress and make new assignments as needed.
3. You may want to tackle additional projects once the first items have been resolved.
4. Repeat the exercise periodically and adjust action plans as necessary.

WORKSHEET 6
RESPONDING TO THE CHANGING UNIVERSE

Company Name: _____Today's Date: _____

Participant's Name: _____

Our Industry: _____

Our Mission: _____

What is one critical change we anticipate?

What are our options and what are the risks and benefits of each?

What option are we considering for implementation?

Who are the stakeholders and what is the impact on them?

What will be the impact throughout the organization?

What are our next steps?

UNIT 7: HOW DO WE REALLY FEEL ABOUT CHANGE?

In today's fast-paced world, the politically correct view of change is often, "Change? I can't get enough of it. I'm a mover and shaker. Bring it on!" Ambivalence about change is interpreted as a sign of weakness, indecision, or worst of all, as being hopelessly out of date. If we believe the talk around the coffee machine, every individual is chomping at the bit to remold, reform, transform and shake things up. Out with the old, in with the new and forge ahead. The desire for change and transformation appears universal.

So what happens when substantive change is proposed? Things begin to vacillate. The word "but" creeps into conversations. The phrase, "Yes, but..." echoes with increased urgency. Change in the abstract is everyone's friend, but when change comes knocking at the door, it often gets a frigid reception.

Change involves a shift in power. It strikes at the heart of self-esteem and can carry implications for promotion, status, job security and personal empire. Change is seen as creating winners and losers. Regardless of the specifics, the specter of change creates an uncertain future. Even if a current proposal has no impact or is beneficial to an individual, a culture of change carries the inherent possibility of future loss.

On the other hand, the absence of change can also leave staff members frustrated and fearful. They may foresee an uncertain future and job loss looming because the organization lacks the ability to adapt and compete. Innovation can be blocked and opportunities lost. A defunct organization means that every employee is a loser.

Through discussion, leadership team members can explore the culture of change in the organization. Misperceptions can be addressed and feedback solicited. The fear of change and the fear of inertia can be assessed and reconciled. A healthy dialog reaps benefits for both team members and the organization overall.

GUIDE TO UNIT 7

Purpose:

This unit examines perceptions about change, the corporate position and the corporate reality.

Objectives:

- Explore personal feelings about change.
- Discuss the official corporate position on change.
- Discuss the corporate realities regarding change.
- Raise issues and suggestions regarding dealing effectively with change in the future.

Process:

1. Select and assign the exercise.
2. Set the ground rule that all opinions are valid and will be respected.
3. Discuss each point, soliciting feedback from individuals.
4. Explore ways in which change can be genuinely supported by the staff.
   (You might have to change in order to make change more acceptable!)
5. Discuss any indicated future activity and implement an Action Plan as needed.

Follow-up:

1. Have progress reports at the next meeting.
2. Assess progress and make new assignments as indicated.
3. Re-assess the response to change, based on the outcome of assigned activities.

WORKSHEET 7
HOW DO WE REALLY FEEL ABOUT CHANGE?

1. How do I feel about change?

   a. Change is wonderful! I can't wait to see what happens next! Bring it on!
   b. I can handle it, most of the time.
   c. I don't want to think about it.
   d. Too much is happening, too fast. I can't keep up.
   e. I can't take it. Things have to go back to the way they were.

2. I think change is occurring:

   a. Faster than ever before
   b. At about the same speed as always
   c. Slower than in the past

3. I think in the foreseeable future:

   a. Change will accelerate.
   b. Change will slow down.
   c. Things will change back to the way they were.
   d. Change will go away.

4. Our corporate assumption is:

   a. Change will slow down or stop.
   b. Change will continue.
   c. Change will accelerate.

5. Our corporate strategy is to:

   a. Ignore change.
   b. Deal with crises as they occur.
   c. Make changes when we are forced to.
   d. Change cautiously.
   e. Anticipate change and move proactively.
   f. Change constantly just for the sake of change.

6. Comparing my attitudes to our corporate strategy:

    a. My perspectives and attitude are fully attuned to the corporate strategy.
    b. I can work with the corporate position but I'm not comfortable with it.
    c. I can't get on board with the corporate position. It is highly stressful to me.
    d. I think the corporate strategy is totally wrong and I feel I have to oppose it.

7. My ideas about dealing with change for the corporation:

UNIT 8: IS INNOVATION A DIRTY WORD?

How much innovation is enough? Is your company leading the industry, along for the ride, or trailing behind? If your company has historically been an industry leader, are you maintaining this position? What is the strategy for staying ahead? If you're not in the vanguard, are you keeping up, or is change accelerating and leaving you behind in the dust?

On the other hand, how much innovation is too much? Is your company changing too radically? Are you changing just for the sake of change? Are you really gaining anything or are you wasting valuable resources?

Beyond the corporate culture, each individual has a personal capacity for innovation. Some are highly creative and thrive on inventing new solutions for emerging challenges. Others prefer slower change or the status quo. Ideally, the corporate culture matches the need for innovation, and leadership team members are individually attuned to this need. A highly innovative individual can be frustrated if the corporate culture is overly conservative. Conversely, an environment of constant innovation can be intolerable for a more cautious team member.

Focus on the speed of innovation demanded by the marketplace, the corporate position relative to this standard and finally, the ability of team members to function effectively within this framework. Effective innovation requires consistency at all three levels. Discuss these factors, individually and collectively. Find and achieve the level of innovation necessary for long term success.

GUIDE TO UNIT 8

Purpose:

The purpose of this unit is to reflect on innovation, the corporate position and the corporate reality, and explore new ideas for promoting innovation.

Objectives:

- Explore personal feelings about innovation.
- Discuss the environment of innovation in the company.
- Discuss the corporate realities regarding change.
- Explore new ideas for promoting innovation.

Process:

1. Select and assign the exercise.
2. Set the ground rule that all opinions are valid and will be respected.
3. Discuss each point, soliciting feedback from individuals.
4. Discuss an appropriate level of innovation for your company.
5. Explore ways in which an appropriate level of innovation can be achieved. (You might have to find an innovative solution in order to innovate!)
6. Discuss any indicated future activity and implement an Action Plan as needed.

Follow-up:

1. Have progress reports at the next meeting.
2. Assess progress and make new assignments as indicated.
3. Re-assess the innovative profile of the company as needed.

WORKSHEET 8
IS INNOVATION A DIRTY WORD?

1. For our company to survive and thrive, our level of innovation must be:
   a. Much higher than we currently are achieving
   b. High, and we're functioning at about the right level
   c. Moderate, and we are ok the way we are
   d. Less than we're currently trying to do

2. I think innovation is:
   a. Absolutely critical to survival today
   b. Useful
   c. Overrated
   d. Nothing but trouble down the road

3. How innovative am I?
   a. I thrive on innovation. There's always a solution and I can invent at least three new ones for any problem.
   b. Once in awhile I can get inspired with a good idea or a new perspective on a problem.
   c. I admire those who come up with innovative solutions; I don't usually have that talent.

4. Our leadership team:
   a. Is highly innovative, always coming up with great ideas to build business
   b. Occasionally has a good new idea
   c. Has a "don't rock the boat, business as usual" attitude
   d. Crushes innovative ideas
   e. Is so innovative that we tend to fix things that aren't broken and break things that are fixed

5. I think our level of innovation:
   a. Is outstanding and we will thrive
   b. Is just right for future survival
   c. Is not adequate for survival
   d. Is too high and we are our own worst enemy

6.   My ideas in the area of innovation are:

7.   I think we should seriously consider:

UNIT 9: FACING FEARS

Fear is a great thing. It keeps us from doing things that quite frankly, are stupid. Thanks to fear, we usually don't try to jump off cliffs, or wrestle grizzly bears. Closer to home, fear can keep us from telling off the Chairman of the Board, or throwing a laptop out of the window when a program malfunctions. Fear is necessary for survival.

On the other hand, fear can keep us from accomplishment and achievement. Fear can immobilize us. We can stubbornly bury our heads in the sand, sing "la, la, la" at the top of our lungs and refuse to face the real music until it's too late. Fear can exist at many levels. We can fear external threats, real or imagined. We can also fear the backlash from pointing out a threat that others are trying mightily to ignore. Regardless, yielding to fear can be a deadly course of action.

What do you fear? What external challenges do you see for the organization? What internal conditions are jeopardizing the effectiveness or survival of the business? What is the probability of their occurrence, and what do you see as the impact? Facing fears is the first step toward addressing and neutralizing threats to the organization. Discuss and share opinions, face fears head on and work toward creating solutions before it is too late.

GUIDE TO UNIT 9

Purpose:

Identify, expose and address critical concerns for the company.

Objectives:

- Identify the threats and issues of concern to the group.
- Assess the level of threat, potential damage and the probability of occurrence.
- Determine key threats.
- Identify strategies for dealing with key threats.
- Implement steps to deal with these.

Process:

1. Select and assign the exercise.
2. Set the ground rule that all opinions are valid and will be respected.
3. Discuss each point, soliciting feedback from individuals.
4. Identify key threats which require attention and/or action.
5. Determine next steps to be taken.
6. Use the Action Plan to implement a response.

Follow-up:

1. Have progress reports at the next meeting.
2. Assess progress and make new assignments as needed.
3. Re-assess the threat, the progress toward abatement and next steps.
4. Periodically repeat the exercise to determine the overall company status, including threats which no longer are relevant and new threats which have emerged.

WORKSHEET 9
FACING FEARS

Fears From External Threats	Probability of Occurrence	Possible Strategies	Next Steps

Fears Due to Internal Issues	Probability of Occurrence	Possible Strategies	Next Steps

UNIT 10: INNOVATIVE USES FOR RESOURCES

Desperate times call for desperate measures. The superspy caught in an impossible trap hooks a few safety pins together, adds a piece of string and somehow disarms the ticking bomb. Wartime rationing led to the creation of mock apple pies out of crackers. The student facing summer school pulls out every last available brain cell and passes the final exam. Necessity indeed is the mother of invention.

Business today is challenging. Finding new uses for resources can lead to new opportunities. Every organization has an abundance of resources. Some are obvious and used daily, others are so familiar they are ignored, and still others are totally unrecognized. It's time to think creatively, to turn things upside down and inside out, to mine every resource for all it's worth. The success of your business can depend on it.

Start with obvious resources. Take time, for example. It's a resource. How can you use it more effectively? How can you be more productive? What wild things can you do with your time that will improve business, that you never thought of before?

What about the familiar? Take a look at your basic product. What else can it be used for? Who else besides your current customers could use it, either as it is, or with modifications? What can you do to it to make it different, new and exciting? Other familiar resources include your facility, equipment, contacts, customers, reputation, etc. How can you repurpose these?

Next, think about unrecognized resources. Consider your staff members. What talents, skills and experience do they have that they aren't currently using? Ask them. You might find a goldmine of talent and opportunity. The IT technician might have a background in voiceovers and is a natural for narrating your webinars. An administrative assistant might have experience as an event planner and can coordinate your grand opening.

Sometimes cleaning house can lead to the discovery of unrecognized resources. You might find domain names you once registered and never used, which fit perfectly with planned future projects. Supplies that are no longer used in one area might be exactly what another area needs. The chair that didn't fit in somcone's new office might fit perfectly for someone else. One area's rejects can be another's treasure.

Reuse, rethink and recycle can lead to a greener business, both environmentally and financially. A creative perspective and taking a fresh look at everything can save money and open up new opportunities for success.

GUIDE TO UNIT 10

Purpose:

This exercise identifies corporate resources which may not be widely known, and to explore innovative uses for the resources at hand.

Objectives:

- Identify all corporate resources, including miscellaneous skills, hobbies, forgotten assets and seemingly useless items.
- Consider alternate uses for these resources, to contribute toward sales, new products, marketing or operational efficiencies.

Process:

1. Select and assign the exercise.
2. Set the ground rule that all opinions are valid and will be respected.
3. Have each team member list all the resources of which they are aware, both the obvious and the obscure. Some categories:
   a. Employee skills: previous experience, professional training, hobbies
   b. Team and employee personal and professional networks and contacts
   c. Company intellectual property, connections, systems
   d. Obvious assets of the company: cash position, fixed assets, inventory, etc.
   e. Forgotten assets: things hiding in corners, etc.
   f. Assets that look like liabilities: overgrown vacant lots, abandoned vehicles, etc.
4. For each resource, note its current direct use.
5. For each asset, consider other ways in which this might be used to build business, create sales, develop or be sold as a new product, help marketing, or improve efficiency.
6. Discuss findings and compare notes.
7. Select areas for further action and implement an Action Plan.

Follow-up:

1. Have progress reports at the next meeting.
2. Assess progress and make new assignments as needed.

WORKSHEET 10
INNOVATIVE USES FOR RESOURCES

Current Resources	Current Uses	Innovative Uses	Next Steps

Newly Identified Resources	Current Uses	Innovative Uses	Next Steps

UNIT 11: CHALLENGING THE COMPETITION

How do we stack up against the competition? No matter how hard we focus on the customer, the reality is that competitors are a permanent part of our universe. We constantly compete for our customer's attention, business and loyalty. A solid book of business today can be snatched in an instant by established or new competitors. Perversely, what can vanish overnight can take years to rebuild. An ongoing assessment of the competition and ongoing strategic positioning is critical to survival.

To challenge the competition, we must know our opponent and our relative position. Where are his strengths? Where are his weaknesses? How do we compare? What market segments do our competitors dominate? What portions of the market are underserved? How can we orient or position ourselves to serve a viable market segment with unmatched excellence? How do we defend our position?

Do not stop with a review of the obvious. Consider innovative options and opportunities. How can you deliver your product most effectively? How can you ramp up quality to new levels? What can you do to totally reinvent the product and create something new and exciting?

Be creative, be clever. There is a time and place for head to head competition, but often greater gains can be made by finessing the marketplace. The willow tree bends, the oak tree breaks. Going around a boulder is far easier than going through it. Think. And do.

GUIDE TO UNIT 11

Purpose:

Take an overview of the company and its competitive position in the marketplace.

Objectives:

- Identify our position in the marketplace.
- Assess opportunities and threats.
- Develop plans to capitalize on opportunities and address threats.

Process:

1. Select and assign the exercise.
2. Have team members individually complete the chart.
3. Discuss the responses.
4. Develop consensus on key points.
5. Identify opportunities for action.
6. Select areas for further action and implement an Action Plan.

Follow-up:

1. Have progress reports at the next meeting.
2. Assess progress and make new assignments as needed.

WORKSHEET 11
CHALLENGING THE COMPETITION

	Competitor I	Our Company	Actions We Can Take
Product Offerings			
Market Positioning			
Market Penetration			
Financial Strength			
Reputation			
Customer Base			
Ability to Innovate			
Strategic Advantages			
Planned Strategic Initiatives			
Other:			

	Competitor 2	Our Company	Actions We Can Take
Product Offerings			
Market Positioning			
Market Penetration			
Financial Strength			
Reputation			
Customer Base			
Ability to Innovate			
Strategic Advantages			
Planned Strategic Initiatives			
Other:			

UNIT 12: CUSTOMERS AND POTENTIAL CUSTOMERS

Change is constant. What a surprise. Most importantly, the needs of your customers are changing. They may require more or less of what you provide, or they may find they no longer need your current products at all. Alternatives are emerging everywhere, with the seductive lure of the "newest" "improved" and "best."

How can you respond to this challenge? How can you restructure this into an opportunity? First, recognize that you have the power to change as well. You can offer the newest and best options and products, not only for your current customers but also for whole new market segments. You can finesse the marketplace.

Consider your current core customers. Who are they? Why do they buy from you? How often do they buy? How much do they buy? What will motivate them to buy more frequently, or buy more product?

Next, consider new potential customers. Who else can you appeal to? How can you capture their attention and motivate them to buy from you? Do you need to modify your product, or your marketing? How can you be more attractive to them than their current supplier?

Brainstorm possibilities. Chart a strategy. A stagnant company is only safe in a stagnant universe. As soon as a competitor, any competitor, makes a move, you are immediately vulnerable. Be proactive. Anticipate change and capture market share.

GUIDE TO UNIT 12

Purpose:

> Explore new potential markets and new opportunities in current markets.

Objectives:

- Identify our position in the marketplace.
- Assess opportunities and threats.
- Develop plans to capitalize on opportunities and address threats.

Process:

1. Select and assign the exercise.
2. Have team members individually complete the chart.
3. Discuss the responses:
    a. Where are the opportunities?
    b. How can we modify our product to reach new customers?
    c. How can we modify our marketing to reach new customers?
    d. Do we have a customer segment that is detrimental to our business?
    e. How can we co-opt these customers into a productive plan?
4. Develop consensus on key points.
5. Discuss opportunities for action.
6. Select areas for further action and implement an Action Plan.

Follow-up:

1. Have progress reports at the next meeting.
2. Assess progress and make new assignments as needed.

WORKSHEET 12
CUSTOMERS AND POTENTIAL CUSTOMERS

	Current Customers	How Can We Increase Sales to Them?	Action Items
Description of the customer			
The products they purchase			
How big is this population?			
How often do they purchase?			
Who competes for this customer?			
Why will this customer buy from us and not our competitors?			
What do we have to do to sell to this customer in the future?			
How expensive is it to keep or gain this customer?			
What negative factors, if any, are associated with this type of customer?			
What is our future strategy for this type of customer?			

	New Potential Customers	How Can We Capture this Market?	Action Items
Description of the customer			
The products they purchase			
How big is this population?			
How often do they purchase?			
Who competes for this customer?			
Why will this customer buy from us and not our competitors?			
What do we have to do to sell to this customer in the future?			
How expensive is it to keep or gain this customer?			
What negative factors, if any, are associated with this type of customer?			
What is our future strategy for this type of customer?			

UNIT 13: NEW PRODUCT ASSESSMENT

Something old, something new…

"Something new" opens up infinite options. Everything is conceivably fair game as you consider new products for the future. Your new product can be a physical item or it can be a service. It might be in your current industry, or in a totally unrelated field. How do you assess the multitude of potential possibilities? Where do you invest your time and resources?

Careful analysis is critical. A successful product must be the best solution to a real problem for a real customer. You are competing not only against your current competitors, but also against any competitors who are already in your new market, as well as competitors who are also seeking to expand into serving the same customer base. You will be investing time, effort and resources. By choosing one option, you will be precluding others. Take a moment to think about new product possibilities. How will the new product fit with your existing product line? Will it add new business or serve existing customers? Does it improve your competitive position in the future? What will be the response of competitors? Consider all possibilities.

Solicit input from all stakeholders. What may be overlooked by some might be obvious to others. Remember that a successful product must be supported by not only customers willing to buy, but also by an effective production process, effective marketing and sales, and sound financials and profit margins. Are you able to sell, produce and deliver the product at a profit? Resolve issues before you begin. Adapt your plans as needed to provide the strongest position for your new product.

Launching a new product can be exciting, invigorating and rewarding. Evaluate your options, plan ahead and seize opportunities!

GUIDE TO UNIT 13

Purpose:

This unit evaluates and compares new product ideas.

Objectives:

- Assess new products in terms of risk and reward.
- Explore positive and negative impacts of proposed products.
- Compare products to each other.
- Identify opportunities to combine the best aspects of several alternative products.

Process:

1. Select and assign the exercise.
2. Have team members individually complete the chart.
3. Discuss the responses:
   a. Where are the opportunities?
   b. Are there any factors which are deal breakers for a product?
   c. How can we innovate and develop a new product that customers really want?
4. Develop consensus on key points.
5. Discuss opportunities for action.
6. Use the Prioritizing Opportunities and Action Plan worksheets as needed.
7. Select areas for further action and implement the Action Plan.

Follow-up:

1. Have progress reports at the next meeting.
2. Assess progress and make new assignments as needed.

WORKSHEET 13
NEW PRODUCT ASSESSMENT

	New Product
Description of the Product	
Is this an additional product or replacement?	
Fully describe the intended customer.	
What is their critical need that is unmet, that our new product meets?	
Why is our product the absolute best solution for the customer's needs?	
How difficult will it be to get to market? What are the problems?	
How will we address these problems?	
What is the financial risk? Is it worth it?	

What other opportunities will this preclude?	
What is the competition for this market?	
What is the upside potential?	
What will be the impact on our current product line?	
What else do we need to research?	
What other things do we need to consider?	
What are our next steps?	

UNIT 14: REVAMPING EXISTING PRODUCTS

Sometimes new markets are there for the taking; it just takes a creative vision to see the hidden potential. How can you take your current products and re-position, re-engineer or re-purpose them to create or seize new market opportunities? The world is filled with creative examples. Fishing lures have become highly desirable hair ornaments. Rubber bands were transformed into collectable bracelets. Years ago, rocks became pets.

Think creatively. What other uses are there for your product? How can you appeal to a new set of customers? What ideas can you borrow from other industries? If you are in a service industry, how can you deliver your core service in a new way?

Don't limit yourself to a few ideas. Explore all possibilities. Don't throw out the outrageous; rather think of how you might incorporate the unexpected into your plans. Combine ideas. Consult individuals outside of your industry. Think about how you might reposition and sell your product to the most unlikely user.

Think beyond the creative idea. Who will be your new competitors? Just because a field is new to you doesn't mean it is an open market. For example, fast food chains expanded into designer coffees, and now compete directly with existing coffee shops. Know why customers will prefer you to existing businesses. Do you offer things that the others don't? Are you more kid-friendly? Is your product application so strange that it's just plain funny? Be ready to compete in the new marketplace.

Repositioning can open up new markets for your existing products. You might find that what is commonplace in your current market is wild, wacky and hugely appealing to a different audience. Look at your products in a new light, and see what opportunities are there for the taking!

GUIDE TO UNIT 14

Purpose:

This unit explores options for refreshing, repurposing and repositioning existing products.

Objectives:

- View current products in light of the current and future market opportunities.
- Consider refreshing, repurposing or repositioning options.
- Evaluation opportunities for the revamped products.
- Identify opportunities to combine the best aspects of several alternative products.

Process:

1. Select and assign the exercise.
2. Have team members individually complete the chart.
3. Discuss the responses:
   a. Where are the opportunities?
   b. Are there any factors which are deal breakers for a product?
   c. How can we innovate and develop a new product that customers really want?
4. Develop consensus on key points.
5. Discuss opportunities for action.
6. Use the Prioritizing Opportunities and Action Plan worksheets as needed.
7. Select areas for further action and implement an Action Plan.

Follow-up:

1. Have progress reports at the next meeting.
2. Assess progress and make new assignments as needed.

WORKSHEET 14
REVAMPING EXISTING PRODUCTS

	Current Product	New Idea I Repurposed/ Repositioned/ Repackaged, etc.	New Idea II Repurposed/ Repositioned/ Repackaged, etc.
Description of the Product			
Intended user			
Intended purpose			
Industry we're borrowing from			
Idea or concept we're borrowing			
Uniqueness or "Wow" Factor			

	Current Product	New Idea I Repurposed/ Repositioned/ Repackaged, etc.	New Idea II Repurposed/ Repositioned/ Repackaged, etc.
Competition/ New competitors			
Costs involved			
Risks involved			
What is the upside potential?			
What will be the impact on our current product line?			
What else do we have to research?			
What are our next steps?			

UNIT 15: GETTING TO THE ROOT OF THE PROBLEM

What is your REALLY BIG PROBLEM? What keeps you awake at night? What are you doing to get out from under its shadow? Big problems cast big shadows, and big shadows can paralyze us. There never seems to be enough time to make headway, and tomorrow seems soon enough to really think about the issues. With every passing "tomorrow" the shadow looms larger and darker.

Now is the time to take a deep breath and attack the problem at its roots. Stare it down; dissect it and identify its most vulnerable points. It's never going to get any easier. Move forward, one step at a time, and cut the problem down to size. Take a look at the component parts and root causes. Then explore the causes underlying the causes. What are the critical elements? What can you do to address these and make progress, no matter how slight it seems? Actions don't have to be big or all-encompassing to be effective. Small changes, well-placed, can yield big results.

Often, listing root causes and actions can reveal new approaches not initially considered. Several seemingly unrelated issues may be effectively addressed by a single action. The problem which is impossible as a whole may be quite manageable once captured on paper and objectively explored. Take time to consider root causes and solutions and cut off your really big problem at the roots.

GUIDE TO UNIT 15

Purpose:

This unit focuses on processes within the organization and options to improve their effectiveness.

Objectives:

- Identify root causes of problems.
- Brainstorm options to address root causes.
- Select alternatives to pursue.
- Set a plan for implementation.

Process:

1. Select and assign the exercise.
2. Have team members complete the chart individually or in teams.
3. Discuss the responses:
    a. What root causes are identified?
    b. What consensus is there on root causes?
    c. What are some options to address the root causes?
    d. Which of these are likely to be most effective in addressing the problem?
4. Plan further action.

Follow-up:

1. Have progress reports at the next meeting.
2. Assess progress and make new assignments as needed.

WORKSHEET 15
GETTING TO THE ROOT OF THE PROBLEM

Our REALLY BIG PROBLEM:

_____

Root causes:

1._____   4. _____

2._____   5. _____

3. _____   6. _____

(Copy these pages if you have more than six root causes)

<u>Underlying</u> causes and solutions

Root cause 1: _____

Underlying causes	Solutions

Root cause 2: _____

Underlying causes	Solutions

Root cause 3: _____

Underlying causes	Solutions

Root cause 4: _____

Underlying causes	Solutions

Root cause 5: _____

Underlying causes	Solutions

Root cause 6: _____

Underlying causes	Solutions

Circle the solutions you want to pursue.

Next steps:

Research:

Trial Implementation:

Other:

UNIT 16: ASSESSING GROWTH OPPORTUNITIES

How do you want to grow? Do you want to vertically integrate within your industry, or increase market penetration? Do you want to franchise your operation or buy a competitor? Do you want to remain the same size but improve profitability? There are many ways to grow. Consider the range of possibilities; you may find that a seemingly unlikely option can be an excellent fit for your business.

Within each growth mode, a whole range of tactical options is available. For example, if you are interested in growing through acquisition, you might consider acquiring a local competitor, or a geographically distant competitor, or you might focus on acquiring an online entity. You may acquire a supplier or a client. Each option has different implications not only for profitability, but also for future opportunities.

Growth is a critical part of business. Select those opportunities and options which fit your plan and position your company for strategic success in the short and long term future.

GUIDE TO UNIT 16

Purpose:

This unit identifies opportunities and actions for future growth.

Objectives:

- Identify the type of growth desired.
- Identify options for achieving this growth.
- Evaluate critical factors relative to the option.
- Determine if future consideration is warranted.

Process:

1. Select and assign the exercise.
2. Have team members complete the chart individually or in groups.
3. Encourage innovative thinking.
4. Discuss the responses:
   a. What opportunities are identified?
   b. Which of these are most viable?
   c. What can the company do to seize the opportunity?

Follow-up:

1. Determine options for further consideration.
2. Assign items areas for further research.
3. Follow up with items at the next meeting.
4. Develop an action plan or revisit the exercise as needed.

WORKSHEET 16
ASSESSING GROWTH OPPORTUNITIES

	Growth Opportunity I	Growth Opportunity II
Type of growth: (Vertical integration, geographic expansion, competitor acquisition, market penetration, new markets, new market segments, profitability enhancement, etc.)		
Description of the growth opportunity		
Description of the tactic under consideration to take advantage of the opportunity		
Downside Risks		
Upside Potential		
Feasibility		

How does this position us for the next 12 months?		
How does this position us for the next 3 to 5 years?		
How does this expand or preclude future options?		
Other considerations:		
Is this worth further consideration?		

Notes:

UNIT 17: THE OPTIONS BRAINSTORM

Sometimes less is more. There are situations that can benefit greatly from a freeform brainstorm, without a lot of structure or complexity. Focus on a single issue. What are your options? What else? What if none of these work out? What will you do then?

Work alone and see what you create, then compare your ideas with others. The range of possibilities is endless. Use options brainstorming when you're facing opportunities or challenges, or when you just want to shake things up. Keep things loose; there are no wrong answers. Let your imagination run free. Face your worst nightmares and create a happy ending. Find wild and outrageous alternatives. Some of them may be more feasible than you think. The future is yours; meet it with creativity!

GUIDE TO UNIT 17

Purpose:

This exercise translates observations into options for action.

Objectives:

- Focus on one observable situation critical to the company.
- Clearly define the opportunity or threat.
- Identify innovative options for addressing the situation.

Process:

1. Select and assign the exercise.
2. State the observable situation you are addressing.
3. Define the underlying opportunity or threat.
4. Have team members complete the form individually or in teams. Don't forget to do the second page.
5. Encourage innovative thinking.
6. Discuss the responses:
    a. What options are most exciting?
    b. Which ones have the best prospects for success?
    c. Which ones are feasible?
7. Plan further action; Use the Prioritizing Opportunities and Action Plan forms.

Follow-up:

1. Have progress reports at the next meeting.
2. Assess progress and make new assignments as needed.

WORKSHEET 17
THE OPTIONS BRAINSTORM

Observation: _____

The opportunity or threat: _____

Options, Part I

List options for addressing the opportunity or threat:

1.

2.

3.

4.

5.

6.

7.

8.

9.

10.

11.

12.

13.

14.

15.

Options, Part II

Look at each option you listed in Part I. For each of these, what can you do if that option doesn't work? List your fallback options below. These must be new ideas; do not repeat any options.

1.

2.

3.

4.

5.

6.

7.

8.

9.

10.

11.

12.

13.

14.

15.

Options, Part III

List any other options that come to mind here:

Options, Part IV

From all the above options, what are your best ideas?

UNIT 18: PRIORITIZING THREATS

Sometimes it seems like we're in the midst of a sea of sharks. Competitors, internal dissention, malfunctioning processes, sales slumps and rising customer expectations can be overwhelming. Resources are always limited. Where do you concentrate your attention and effort? What fires do you fight first? Jumping from one crisis to another is confusing and exhausting, and in the end, nothing is really resolved. Facing threats head-on can lead to focus, action, and resolution. But where do you start? Which threat do you address first?

Pause for a moment and take stock of the sea of sharks surrounding your business. List them all. Examine them one by one. What is the core of the threat? How urgent is this? How does it rank among all the threats you have listed?

Consider how you might address the threat. What will it take to eliminate, confine or neutralize it? What is the cost in time, effort and other resources? You might find that you need to address your most urgent threat at any cost. Or you may choose to tackle a less urgent threat that can be eliminated rather quickly and easily.

Regardless of where you start, each threat you eliminate gives you additional capacity to focus on the remaining threats, as well as your ongoing operations. Take stock, take action and take control of your business!

GUIDE TO UNIT 18

Purpose:

This unit guides the team in identifying, assessing and prioritizing threats.

Objectives:

- Identify threats as seen by team members.
- Rank the threats on the basis of urgency.
- Assess the costs associated with addressing the threat.
- Determine priorities to move forward.

Process:

1. Select and assign the exercise.
2. Have team members complete the top section of the form individually or in teams.
3. Compare responses and develop a single ranked list of threats, based on input from all team members.
4. Transfer the items in this composite list to the grid on the bottom of the sheet.
5. Have team members complete the rest of the grid, assessing difficulty, cost and time commitments.
6. Add the numeric values. A low sum indicates high urgency and low costs; a high sum indicates the opposite.
7. Discuss the response.
8. Plan further action; Use the Action Plan form.

Follow-up:

1. Have progress reports at the next meeting.
2. Assess progress and make new assignments as needed.

WORKSHEET 18
PRIORITIZING THREATS

Key Threats, Not Ranked	Urgency Ranking 1=most urgent 10=least urgent

Consider the difficulty of addressing each threat, as well as the cost, impact and time commitment. Use the form on the next page as needed, to capture specific thoughts and ideas.

Threats Ranked from 1 - 10	Rank	Anticipated complexity 1=easy 10=hard	Anticipated financial cost 1=cheap 10=expensive	Anticipated time commitment 1=quick 10=extensive	Impact on future position 1=good 10=poor	Sum of rank, complexity, cost, impact and time #s	Act Now? Y/N
	1						
	2						
	3						
	4						
	5						
	6						
	7						
	8						
	9						
	10						

Threat: _____   Urgency Ranking: _____

What do we need to do to address this?

How difficult is it to address?

Will this eliminate, neutralize or decrease the threat?

What is the impact on our future position?

How much time will this take?

What is the financial cost?

What other resources are required?

What other options do we have to address this threat?

UNIT 19: PRIORITIZING OPPORTUNITIES

Are you facing too much of a good thing? Do you have multiple options, all of which are promising? Just as a sea of threats can be immobilizing, so too can an abundance of opportunities. Which ones should you pursue?

Multiple factors can enter into the analysis. Consider the urgency – is there a deadline or a window of time in which you must act? Which will have the best payoff? Is the payoff worth the effort? Which options will best position you for the future? What risks are involved? How will your actions today impact your future position?

Some opportunities will preclude others. Consider and weigh these interactions. The choices you make will set the course for future growth and opportunities. Envision the future. What steps do you need to take now to position your business for tomorrow's customers? Which opportunities will lead you to that position, and which ones will provide short term gains but lead you away from your strategic plan?

Consider the resources you have. Do you have the resources you need to act effectively on the opportunity? What will be the impact on the rest of your business? If the opportunity does not turn out the way you expect, will you have the resources to continue to operate? Consider your available personnel and management resources. Do key staff members support this opportunity? If not, why not?

Look carefully at your opportunities. Consider the risks as well as the potential rewards. Evaluate your resources. Check your strategic direction. When it looks good, move ahead and act!

GUIDE TO UNIT 19

Purpose:

This unit guides the team in assessing and prioritizing opportunities.

Objectives:

- Identify opportunities as seen by management team members.
- Rank the opportunities on the basis of potential.
- Assess the costs associated with taking advantage of opportunities.
- Determine priorities to move forward.

Process:

1. Select and assign the exercise.
2. Have team members complete the top section of the form individually or in groups.
3. Use the questions on page 2 of the worksheet as necessary to focus your analysis.
4. Compare responses and develop a single ranked list of opportunities, based on input from all team members.
5. Transfer the items in this composite list to the grid on the bottom of the sheet.
6. Have team members complete the rest of the grid, assessing difficulty, cost and time commitments.
7. Add the numeric values. A low sum indicates high potential and low costs; a high sum indicates the opposite.
8. Discuss the responses.
9. Plan further action; Use the Action Plan form.

Follow-up:

1. Have progress reports at the next meeting.
2. Assess progress and make new assignments as needed.

WORKSHEET 19
PRIORITIZING OPPORTUNITIES

Opportunities, Not Ranked	Urgency 1=must act now 10=indefinite opportunity

Consider each opportunity, including the cost, impact and time commitment. Use the form on the next page as needed, to capture specific thoughts and ideas.

Opportunities ranked by urgency	Rank	Anticipated complexity 1=easy 10=hard	Anticipated financial cost 1=cheap 10=expen-sive	Anticipated time commitment 1=quick 10=exten-sive	Impact on future position/ risks 1=good 10=poor	Sum of rank, complexity, cost, impact and time #s	Act Now? Y/N
	1						
	2						
	3						
	4						
	5						
	6						
	7						
	8						
	9						
	10						

Opportunity: _____   Urgency Ranking: _____

What do we need to do to take advantage of this?

What is the window of opportunity? Is there a deadline on this opportunity?

How much effort will it take?

How much time will this take?

What is the financial cost?

What other resources are required?

What are the risks?

What is the immediate impact?

How does this position us for the future?

UNIT 20: THE WORST POSSIBLE EXERCISE

Just for a moment, put yourself into your customers' shoes. Now imagine. What is the worst possible experience your customers could have with your company? What would it look like if everything went totally wrong, if your staff did everything they could to frustrate, anger and disgust your customers? What would your product be, if it were so bad that customers decided on the spot never ever to buy from you again? What policies would you have in place that would make customers flee to the search engines, looking for a friendlier company? Would your website be impossible to navigate? Would your phones never be answered? Would complaints never be resolved?

Now consider the radical opposite to every item on your list. Don't just stop at what is acceptable. Acceptable is the absolute minimum baseline that customers today demand. You're aiming for much more. Instead, envision the extraordinary, where everything is beyond perfect, where everyone who encounters your company is dazzled and speechless.

You're aiming for "Wow." You're aiming for an experience so extraordinary that people can't stop talking about you. That's word of mouth advertising. That's your reputation. That's your ultimate return on investment.

Sometimes leaders view excellence as not worth the cost. But excellence can yield results which no amount of marketing can produce. Customer retention becomes a given. The investment in infrastructure and service elevates your product to new levels and sets you far apart from the competition. You have "Wow."

The extraordinary does not have to cost a fortune. Capable staff, well trained, with a positive, "can do" attitude goes a long way toward establishing excellence. Make your business a joy to work with. Then, when you've achieved this, continue to improve. Strive to rise higher. Competitors are always right behind you. Stay far ahead of the pack. Be the best thing to happen to every customer, every day.

GUIDE TO UNIT 20

Purpose:

This unit encourages team members to creatively focus on unrivaled excellence.

Objectives:

- Define the worst possible product, service or situation.
- Define the most extraordinary product, service or situation.
- Determine what you need to do to provide an extraordinary customer experience.

Process:

1. Select and assign the exercise.
2. Identify the product, process or service you are examining. This exercise can be done for the company overall, or for one specific area.
3. Fill in additional categories as appropriate in the left column.
4. Fill in the "Worst Possible" column with the worst that could happen.
5. Fill in the "Best Possible" column with the extraordinary opposite.
6. Fill in the column describing how your company can be or produce the "Best Possible."

Follow-up:

1. Use the Action Plan forms in this book to translate your findings to action.
2. Periodically repeat the activity to identify new opportunities.

WORKSHEET 20
THE WORST POSSIBLE EXERCISE

Area	What is the worst possible scenario	What is the radical opposite: (the ultimate best possible)	What can we do to be the best possible?
Product			
Customer Service			
Marketing Effort			
Timeliness			
Follow-up			
Complaint Resolution			
Website			
Telephones			

Areas You Define	What is the worst possible scenario	What is the radical opposite: (the ultimate best possible)	What can we do to be the best possible?
Area:			
Area:			
Area:			
Area:			
Area:			
Area:			
Area:			
Area:			

CONCLUSION

Constant transformation is an integral part of today's business environment. Leadership teams need to efficiently and effectively assess opportunities and threats and respond quickly and decisively. Often action is demanded before complete information is available. There are risks in acting too impulsively, and risks in excessive conservatism.

The capacity to innovate, invent and implement has never been more critical. Teams must depend on their collective experience and talent to develop solutions that are greater than the sum of the parts. There are huge challenges ahead for the business community, and there are huge opportunities. Focus, organize and be ready to seize the future!

APPENDIX I: ACTION AND ACCOUNTABILITY

Planning, ideas and goals are a waste of time, unless they are supported by action. Until you do something, you have accomplished nothing. You may encounter obstacles, and may change course or even abandon a project, but even these outcomes represent progress – you know what doesn't work and you can tackle the situation from a new angle, with new knowledge you have gained through experience.

An action plan has several key components. Responsibility for implementing the plan needs to rest with an individual. This project leader needs to know they are responsible, and needs to have the authority to act and make relevant decisions. This leader also needs the support of management and the organization. Adequate resources of all types need to be budgeted and assigned. A definite goal and timetable need to be set, and these must be supported by management and the responsible individual. To keep the project on course, periodic progress reports should be given, including actions and accomplishments to date as well as any problems or unexpected delays.

Documenting the goals, assignments and timetable can help keep the team and the project on course. Set a direction, define a project, document it and take action to energize your organization.

Guide to Appendix I

Purpose:

This form documents a plan of action, assigns accountability and tracks activity.

Objectives:

- Summarize a plan of action including its goals, staff assignments, progress and outcome.
- Provide a mechanism for accountability and mid-course evaluation.
- Keep group participants focused on the action until completion or modification.

Process:

1. Complete the worksheet, assigning a project leader and any support staff.
2. Ensure the responsible individuals understand and support the plan, timetable and course of action.

Follow-up:

1. Have progress reports at the next meeting.
2. Assess progress and make new assignments as needed.

WORKSHEET APPENDIX I
ACTION AND ACCOUNTABILITY

The challenge or opportunity: _____

The assignment: _____

_____

Date assigned: _____   First report date: _____   Date due: _____

Desired outcome: _____

Project leader: _____

Project team members:: _____ ____ ____

_____ ____ _____

Other support staff: _____

_____

Resources required and authorized:

_____

_____

Project leader's scope of authority: _____ _____

Status report dates	Expected Progress	Actual Progress	Comments

Other comments:

Outcome: _____

Follow up or next steps: _____

APPENDIX II: TRACKING CURRENT PROJECTS

Don't lose track of your projects. It is discouraging and demoralizing when an individual or team takes the time and effort to work on a project, only to discover that leadership has forgotten about the assignment and has moved on to other things. It is equally frustrating when leaders assume a project is progressing as assigned, only to find that the responsible individual has forgotten or abandoned it. An accidentally abandoned project wastes time, money and other resources.

Keep a list of assigned projects and review this list regularly. If circumstances change and a project needs to be redirected or discontinued, inform everyone and ensure the change is understood. Keep notes on any changes or important discussions.

GUIDE TO APPENDIX II

Purpose:

This form tracks the team's progress on current projects.

Objectives:

- List and track all open action item projects for the team.
- Ensure projects are not sidetracked.
- Promote accountability and assistance when needed.

Process:

1. Use the worksheet to list all action items pending for the team.
2. Review all items weekly and not any critical issues in "Comments."
3. Use the form to promote accountability and project completion.

Follow-up:

1. Update the report as necessary.
2. Add new assignments and remove completed assignments.

WORKSHEET APPENDIX II
TRACKING CURRENT PROJECTS

Action Plan Item	Assigned to	Date Assigned	Due Date	Comments

TRACKING CURRENT PROJECTS

Expanded notes and comments:

Date	Project	Expanded Notes and Comments

APPENDIX III: BUBBLE DIAGRAMS

Thoughts are not always linear. Even though we write and drive in relatively straight lines, we are creative creatures, and our thoughts and ideas often bounce about, creating wild linkages and leading into unexpected paths. Bubble diagrams celebrate our erratic thought processes. Here, anything goes. One idea can generate dozens more, or sit alone. Linkages and relationships between ideas can be captured and expanded. Ideas can flow off the paper; you can color outside the lines.

If bubbles aren't your thing, play with other shapes. Doodle, scribble, and capture whatever comes to mind. Then sit back and see what emerges. Are there new relationships you didn't see before? Are there unexpected problems or unexpected solutions? Has a path emerged to get you from where you are to where you want to be?

Share your ideas with others, and go back to the drawing board. Get inspired by their insights and new perspectives. Compare results and combine your efforts. See what new ideas you can generate just by thinking outside the lines.

GUIDE TO APPENDIX III

Purpose:

This worksheet can be used to encourage innovative thinking and problem solving.

Objectives:

- Draw connections and linkages between ideas.
- Explore innovative solutions.

Process:

1. Select and assign the exercise.
2. Put a challenge, opportunity or idea in one of the center bubbles.
3. What other idea does this generate? Write this in an adjacent bubble and connect the bubbles with an arrow.
4. Build off either bubble and generate additional thoughts, connecting them with arrows.
5. Add more bubbles if necessary.
6. A bubble can be attached to more than one other bubble.
7. Review the sheet to see if any ideas merit further exploration.
8. Take the best ideas and start another bubble diagram with that idea in the center.
9. When you have an idea you want to pursue, incorporate it into one of the other exercises in this series.

Follow-up:

1. Utilize other exercises in this series to develop the idea into an actionable item.
2. Repeat the exercise as needed to generate additional ideas.

WORKSHEET APPENDIX III
BUBBLE DIAGRAMS

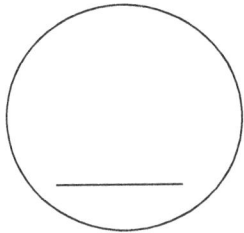

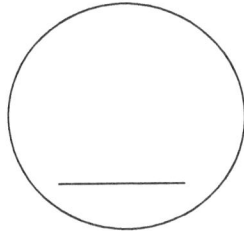

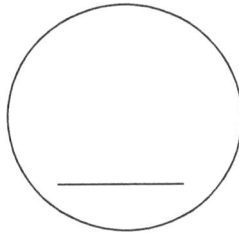

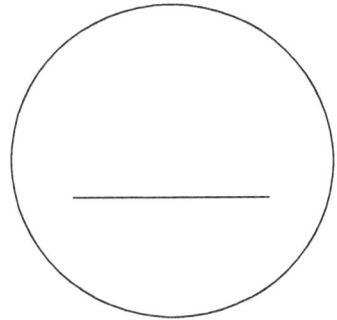

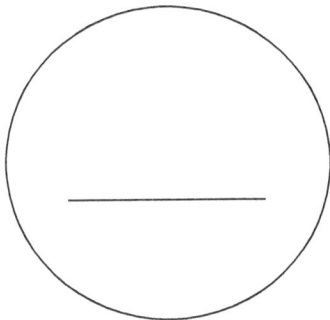

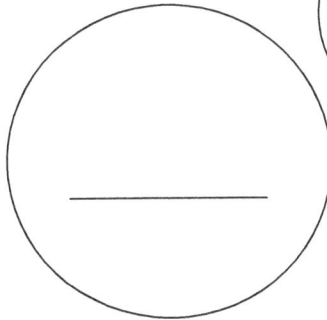

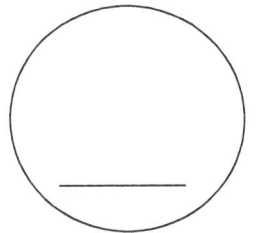

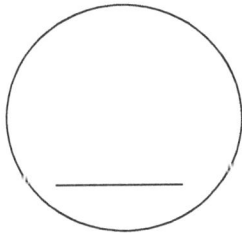

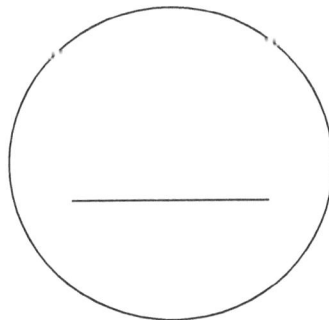

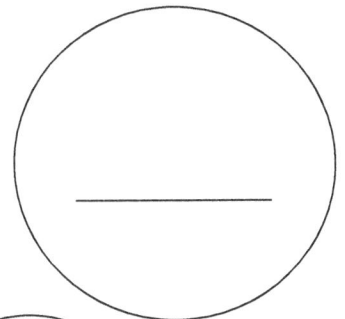

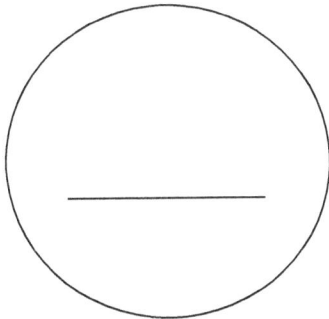

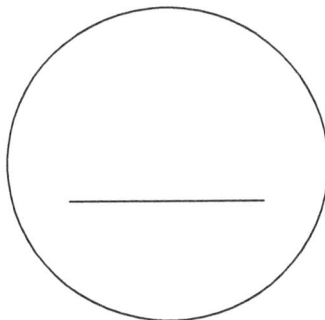

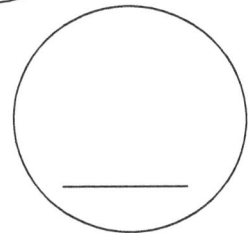

"Bubble" Diagrams
For Those Who Find Bubbles Too Ordinary

Add your own shapes to express your ideas!

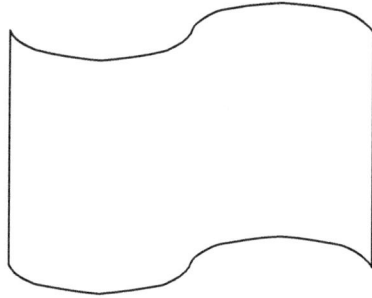

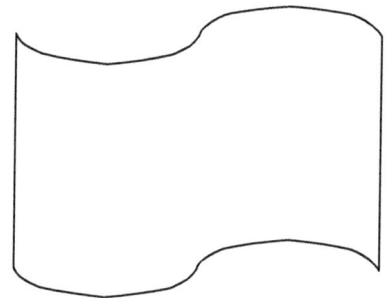

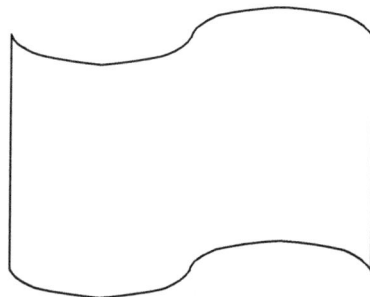

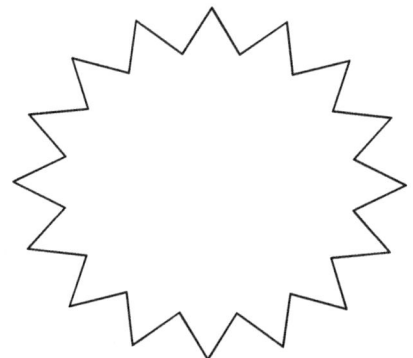

ABOUT THE AUTHOR

Ellen M. Huxtable is the owner of Advantage Business Concepts, a firm specializing in creative, practical business solutions. She has assisted businesses in a wide range of industries, including health care, amusement, technology and service firms. Ellen has presented programs at national, regional and local management seminars, and teaches business programs for Waubonsee Community College.

Ellen is the founder and coordinator of multiple forums for business owners, including mastermind groups, open networking groups and training groups. She has created several proprietary networking processes including "321 Contact!" which is a networking system based on giving, and "I'm Looking For," which is an expedited networking process. Ellen is also the co-founder of the CEO Seminar Series which highlights successful businesses, and Growth Groups, a strategic process for significant business growth.

Ellen serves on the advisory board for the College of DuPage Small Business Development Center as well as the Junior Achievement of Chicago Western Region Board. She is a director at the Elgin Technology Center and a member of the Fermi National Accelerator Laboratory Community Advisory Group.

Ellen received her Masters of Management (MBA) degree from the Kellogg Graduate School of Management, Northwestern University.

ADDITIONAL RESOURCES
FROM ADVANTAGE BUSINESS CONCEPTS

Advantage Business Concepts provides a wide range of creative, practical solutions for businesses. Seminars, presentations and workshops focus on immediate challenges and offer new perspectives and creative ideas for success. Our mastermind groups draw upon the collective expertise of non-competing peers to provide new insights for growth and profitability. Customized support offered to individual businesses addresses challenges in strategic positioning, operations and process development.

Clients include business leaders, corporate management teams, professional organizations, chambers of commerce and not-for-profit organizations. Visit our website, www.advantage-biz.com for information on services, publications and more. Act now to take advantage of creative and innovative solutions from Advantage Business Concepts.